Printed and Published in Great Britain by D. C. THOMSON & CO., LTD.,
185 Fleet Street, London EC4A 2HS.
© D. C. THOMSON & CO., LTD., 1986.
ISBN 0 85116 376 9

# NIGHT MOVES

H'm! That's interesting. It's bad to waken a sleep-walker.

ALL ABOUT SLEEP WALKING

LATER—
Dennis, you've been bad today! Off to bed without any supper!

SOON—
Psst! OK, Gnasher —let's go!

ZZZ!

ZZZ!

Look, Dad! They're sleep-walking!

SUSPICIOUS

Better not waken them, Dad. You know what they say about sleep-walking.

Grr! I'm sure they're just pretending! But I can't take the chance!

BACK IN THE BEDROOM—
It worked like a dream! 'Night, 'night, Gnasher!

Gnight!

NEXT DAY—
It's, OK Gnasher—we can raid the larder! Dad's in slumberland!

SNOOZE

THEN—

Gulp! Now Dad's sleep-walking—or is he?

Wake him up, Mum!

I'd better not. Dennis! You know what they say about sleep-"whacking"!

**HOW TO MAKE A MENACE**

LOOK—HE CAN DO THE TEXAS TWIRL!

HE'S ALSO A GOOD SHOT!

POP! POP!

THAT'S NOT WHAT I MEAN BY A GUN-DOG!

ENTER, SOPPY WALTER—

MY DAD'S WANTING TO SELL ONE OF OUR GUN-DOGS.

WATCH HIM RETRIEVE THIS DUMMY DUCK.

GUN-DOGS HAVE TO BRING BACK BIRDS.

HUH! GNASHER COULD EASILY BRING BACK BIRDS!

NOW, HOW MUCH DO YOU WANT FOR YOUR CLEVER DOG?

YAHOO! YIPPEE!

CLUCK! CLUCK!

HOW'S THAT? GNASHER BROUGHT IN MORE BIRDS THAN THAT PESKY RETRIEVER!

HE'S BEEN IN MY HEN-HOUSE! I SHALL INFORM THE AUTHORITIES OF THIS OUTRAGE!

CLUCK! CLUCK! CLUCK! CLUCK!

SO—

GUN-DOG WANTED FOR CREATING A PUBLIC NUISANCE

# THAT'S YOUR LOT

ONLY ONE THING CAN FRIGHTEN THE MENACE—

IT'S GRANNY'S FAMOUS SLIPPER—THE DEMON WHACKER!....

MADE WITH GENUINE ELEPHANT HIDE!

SO—

Tell us a story, Dad. Tell us about the start of the Demon Whacker!

Once upon a time, when I was a lad, Granny took me to an auction sale...

Now behave, and speak when you're spoken to. Children should be seen and not heard.

Yes, Mama.

AUCTION SALE

DAD AS A LAD

Any bids for lot 29?

I'll ask Mama for a sweetie.

LOT 32

Lot 29, sold to the dear little chap in the sailor suit!

Please may I speak, 'Mama?

Eh?

BOP!

LOT 32

Here you are, Madam—lot 29.

Goodness knows where we're going to put a stuffed elephant!

LOT 29

We're nearly home.

PANT!

I suppose we could keep it in the conservatory.

RUMBLE!

Eek! Now what are we going to do with it?

CRUMP!

This is a nice bit of leather, Missus. Mind if I make a few suggestions?

Please do, my man!

The saddler covered this 3-piece suite, which has lasted for nigh on fifty years—and, with the odd pieces of hide, he made the Demon Whacker—which is going to last even longer!

Ooer!

TREMBLE

# WHAT A DUST-UP!

WHACK!
WHOP!
WHUMP!
WHACK!
WHOWK!

SOUNDS AS IF DENNIS HAS BEEN NAUGHTY AGAIN—

BUT—

WHACK!
WHOP!
WHUMP!
WHAP!
WHUP!
WHAMP!

Heh-heh! Fooled you, readers! Bet you thought I was getting a whacking!

INSIDE—

Granny's entered for the annual char-lady's rug-beating contest!

WHOP!

WHAP!

Whew! I'll have to get in some more training if I'm going to beat Aggie Blenkinsop from across the road.

See if you can get me a dumb-bell. I want to do some weight-lifting to strengthen my arm.

LATER—

This is the only dumb-bell I could get, Granny!

SMIFFY FROM BASH ST.

Never mind he'll do!

Up! Down! Up! Down!

LATER—

Now I'm all set!

FLEX

AT THE CONTEST—

WHAP!

WHOP!

WHOP!

They're off!

DISASTER! GRANNY'S CARPET BEATER COLLAPSES UNDER THE STRAIN—

What'll I do?

I've an idea, Granny!

ONE QUICK DASH HOME LATER—

Here's the Demon Whacker, Granny!

Good thinking, Dennis, lad!

THEN—

Amazing! Granny's broken the world-record, and she's still going strong!

# PLAIN SAILING

Yo-ho-ho! I must enter for that, Gnasher! Let's go home and find my old model yacht.

ON THE WAY HOME—

Snigger! How do you like my super new yacht, "Evening Cloud"? It's going to win the race easily!

Huh! We'll see!

AT HOME—

My old yacht's in here somewhere!

DENNIS'S TOY BOX

PRIVATE

Bah! It looks like the wreck of the Hesperus!

The moths have had a feed off the sails and you've been chewing the hull, Gnasher!

SORRY

I'll just have to build another yacht. Ah—just the job! But first I'd better remove that fruit.

Chomp! Chomp! Hey! There's Dad's fishing jacket—it'll supply nice sails for our model!

IT DOES—

Now to launch this beauty and try her out before the race!

AT THE POND—

Bah! We'll never beat Walter's yacht now!

Idea!

BLEWP!

BUT SHORTLY—

Golly! Granny's "Demon Whacker" slipper and a copy of The Beano! Good thinking, Gnasher!

AT THE RACE—

Beano

The winner! Dennis's—er—yacht takes the £20 first prize!

LATER—

FRESH FRUIT AND NEW BOWL

NEW JACKET

MINT LUMPS

CRUNCH!

Well, I think they're all happy, and I still have enough money left for sweets!

# WATCH THE  BIRDIE

THIS IS ANOTHER OF MY PETS, READERS— JOEY THE BUDGIE. HE'S A REAL MENACE, TOO!

HE SPEAKS—

SQUEAK! WALTER IS A SOPPY DRIP!

—ENJOYS A BATH—IN DAD'S SOUP PLATE—

GET THAT DREADFUL BIRD OUT OF THERE!

DENNIS

—HE ALSO RINGS HIS BELL!

TRING! TRING!

THANKS, DAD!

LATER~

CARE TO VISIT MY AVIARY, DENNIS?

IN WALTER'S AVIARY ~

I'M GOING TO WIN THE RED CARD AT THE BIRD SHOW TODAY! THAT'S THE CARD THAT'S GIVEN TO THE TOP BIRD, YOU KNOW.

I BET MY ENTRY TAKES THE RED CARD!

TITTER! THAT MOTH-EATEN BUDGIE WON'T TAKE THE RED CARD!

BIRD SHOW

SNIFF! RATHER A SCRUFFY SPECIMEN!

YERROWP!

NIP

I MUST GET ANOTHER ENTRY TO TAKE THE RED CARD.

DISQUALIFIED

YOU'RE GOOD AT BIRD IMPERSONATIONS, GNASHER

SO~

I SUSPECT A TRICK, SO I'LL GIVE THE RED CARD TO WALTER'S BIRD OF PARADISE IN THE NEXT CAGE.

BIRD OF PARADISE

EXTREMELY RARE ANDALUSIAN GNASHING VULTURE

FIRST PRIZE

BIRD OF PARADISE

I TOLD YOU MY ENTRY WOULD TAKE THE RED CARD!

WE ARE THE CHAMPIONS!

BIRD OF PARADISE

GNASH! GNASH!

# 'KEEPING' 'COOL'!

It's a hot day, Dennis! Switch on the fan!

Pant! Ok, Granny.

BUT SOON—

Bah! The fan's gone "phut"!

PHUT!

Go down to the shop and get two cool ice-lollies.

Ok, Granny!

Two ice-lollies please, Toni!

Better hurry home before they melt!

SLURPSH!

ALAS—

Gasp! Sorry, Granny, the lollies melted!

Pah! Let's go for a paddle!

AT THE PADDLING POOL—

Aah! That's better!

BUT—

BLEWRP!

Move over, folks! This is the day the pool gets cleaned!

I've got an idea!

LATER—

SWISH!

GRANNY'S WIELDING THE DEMON WHACKER! HAS DENNIS BEEN A BAD BOY?

NO—

Lovely, Granny! I'll take over in another five minutes!

WAFT

COOLING BREEZE

# FANGS A LOT!

THE LOCAL VET IS GIVING DENNIS'S CLASS A LECTURE ON CARE OF PETS —

—And I'm going to give a prize for the dog with the cleanest fangs!

Psst! Hear that, Gnasher?

SO—

You must clean your fangs every day, if you're going to win the "Happiest Snarl Contest".

THEN—

Agh! I knew that dog would go mad some day!

It's OK, Dad! Gnasher's just getting ready for the "Happiest Snarl Contest".

LATER, WALTER SEES GNASHER'S FANGS—

Hm! Gnasher's teeth are so bright—he's sure to win!

SO—

Here, Gnasher have a sweetie for being a good doggie!

YUMSH!

CHOMPSH!

AT THE CONTEST—

Snigger! That liquorice sweet worked a treat!

Ugh! Disgusting!

Foo-Foo is the winner!

Rotten cheat!

ZOP!

Heh-Heh! Foo-Foo's not got anything to smile about now!

# BOWLED OVER

## UNBELIEVA"BOWL" USES FOR GNASHER'S DOG BOWLS

THIS IS DENNIS'S MUM'S DRESSING TABLE—

... BUT THE JAR OF VANISHING CREAM HAS VANISHED—

Bah! This vanishing cream doesn't make the sting vanish! I've just had six of the best from Granny's Demon Whacker!

THROB!

VANISHING CREAM

THE WHACKER MUST GO

DOWN WITH THE DEMON

Gnasher's a great chewer! He'll get rid of The Whacker for me!

ONE OF MUM'S VELVET SLIPPERS

Chew up The Demon Whacker, Gnasher!

GNASH!

Ooer! Gnasher's sprained his jaw and The Whacker's still as good as new!

THEN—

This'll get rid of it!

BUT—

SCUFFLE!

Hey! Get this pesky thing out of my burrow!

Sorry, Mr Mole!

NEXT—

Snigger! This'll squash The Whacker flat!

RUMBLE!

BUT—

CRUMP!

Ok, you win! I'll just have to try being a good boy in future!

GLARE

A LIKELY TALE!

HEY, PORTER, LEND A HAND HERE.

GASP! IT'S TOO HEAVY FOR US!

MY TRAIN IS AT PLATFORM FIVE!

GNERK!

OOF! THERE'S MORE MONEY BEING A CABBY. AND YOU GET BIGGER TIPS. I'LL GET THE BOYS!

HEY! CURLY, PIE-FACE, ANDY. GO GET YOUR CARTIES.

"THE CARTYCABS" ARE READY TO ROLL, DENNIS!

A FINE BODY OF MEN!

CARTY CABS

SOON— CABBY!

YOU TAKE THAT ONE, CURLY!

THE SWEET SHOP, CABBY AND DON'T SPARE THE HORSES!

HOP ON, SIR— BUT GENTLY!

CARTY CABS

THAT'S ONE CARTY GONE

CRUNCH!

THEN— CABBY!

YOU TAKE THAT ONE, PIE-FACE!

BUT— YOU'D NO BUSINESS PINCHING THAT BOX IN THE FIRST PLACE, PIE-FACE! I WANT IT FOR FIRE-WOOD.

ULP! SORRY, DAD!

CARTY CABS

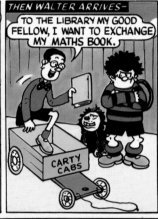

THEN WALTER ARRIVES—

TO THE LIBRARY MY GOOD FELLOW, I WANT TO EXCHANGE MY MATHS BOOK.

CARTY CABS

I'LL GET HIM THERE QUICKLY AND MAYBE GET A BIG TIP!

COOOAAHH! WHAT A SUPER TOFFEE-APPLE! SLURP!

I SAY, DRIVER, KEEP YOUR EYE ON THE ROAD.

NOTHING TO WORRY ABOUT, SIR—AAAH— WHO PUT THAT BRICK THERE?

CLONK!

DENNIS LANDED A BIG TIP OK, READERS—A RUBBISH TIP!

I WANT MY MUMMY!

RUBBISH TIP

I WON'T CHARGE YOU ANYTHING FOR THIS TOUR OF THE LOCAL BEAUTY SPOTS, SIR!

# STORY...

Hm! Those reducing exercises don't seem to be working, Gnasher!

My ancestors were performing dogs. Maybe I could join a circus!

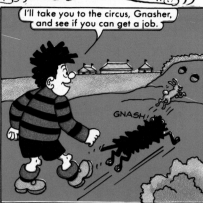

I'll take you to the circus, Gnasher, and see if you can get a job.

GNASH!

Oops! Poor old Gnasher's got stuck in the rabbit's burrow!

Hm! You're a bit bent! Never mind—have an aniseed ball. That'll make you feel better.

CRAMPED

Yummy! I'll do anything for an aniseed ball!

AT THE CIRCUS—

Have we any volunteers for the human cannon-ball?

Here's Gnasher's big chance!

A brave dog has volunteered!

Slurp! An aniseed ball!

BOOM!

BUT GNASHER'S BENT LIKE A BOOMERANG, SO HE COMES BACK—

THUMP!

Fantastic! What an act! The Barking Boomerang! I have here a contract!

Good! That last thump has got Gnasher back to his old self!

Gnasher's decided not to join the circus, readers. I'm glad, and I bet you are, too!

TEARING UP HIS CONTRACT

SO–

SNIGGER! I'LL SWEEP IT UNDER THE RUG!

THAT'S MUCH TIDIER.

OUTSIDE THE TV STUDIO–

THAT'S THE JOB FOR YOU, PUP-O'-MINE!

HANDSOME VIGOROUS DOG WANTED FOR DOG FOOD AD.

APPLY

HANDSOME AND VIGOROUS

SOON–

BAH! WALTER AND FOO-FOO ARE GETTING SCREEN-TESTED FIRST!

SLOPPO DOG CEREAL

I'LL SOON GET RID OF FOO-FOO!

SLOPPO DOG CEREAL

SLOP!

THAT'S THE DOG FOR US!

CAMERA I

PERFECT, GNASHER!

SLOP! SLOP!

CEREAL FOR DOGS

CAMERA 2

SLOPPO

AFTER THE FILMING IS FINISHED–

RIGHT–WE'LL TAKE GNASHER'S WAGES NOW.

CERTAINLY, DENNIS.

THERE'S GNASHER'S WAGES, A YEAR'S SUPPLY OF "SLOPPO"!

2 DOZ SLOPPO | 2 DOZ SLOPPO | 2 DOZ SLO

2 DOZ SLOPPO | 2 DOZ SLOPPO | 2 DOZ SLO

GASP!

2 DOZ SLOPPO

BACK HOME–

OH! I CAN'T GET INTO HIS ROOM AGAIN!

SHOVE

DENNIS'S ROOM

BAH! THIS PLACE IS EVEN MORE LIKE A DOG'S BREAKFAST NOW!

SLOP! SLOP!

# WHAT A

CARD

IS DAD READING A HORROR STORY?

SHUDDER

Agh!

NO, IT'S JUST DENNIS'S LATEST SCHOOL REPORT CARD!

Pah! Disgraceful! You'd better improve!

And that stupid brute of a dog is just as bad!

NEXT DAY—

Sigh! Ah, well, back to school!

DOG TRAINING SCHOOL

GNASHER'S GOING TO SCHOOL, TOO!

SUMS CLASS—

$x + y = 2$

$2 - x = y$

I can't get the hang of this algebra.

SOON—

What is the date of the Battle of Bannockburn?

Er—1492?

LOOKS AS IF DENNIS IS IN FOR ANOTHER BAD REPORT!

LATER—

Would you care to look at this report card, Dad?

REPORT CARD

THIS PUPIL IS CLEVER, INTELLIGENT, ALERT, WELL-BEHAVED AND SHOWS GREAT PROMISE.

YOURS TRULY,

Teacher

Well done, lad— here's 10p!

OUTSIDE—

Thanks for the loan of your report card, Gnasher!

You saved me from a whacking, faithful pal! You deserve that bone I bought you!

BUTCHER

# WHAT A PET

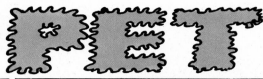

Must enter for that!

TOWN HALL —TODAY!
CHILDREN'S
PET SHOW
FOR
UNUSUAL
PETS ONLY

Hm! I think you're unusual, Gnasher, but to most folk you're just an ordinary dog!

FOR UNUSUAL PETS O

I'll go to the pet shop and see if they've any unusual pets.

PET SHOP

Look at my unusual pet, Dennis. It's a chameleon. It changes colour to suit its surroundings.

Hold it up to Gnasher and see what colour it turns.

GNASH!
Heh! Heh! It's turned white with fear!

Isn't he sweet? He likes me already! How much?
SNAP!

Ten pounds for the croc.!
Aw, boo! I don't even have ten pence!

BACK HOME—
Looks like I'll miss the show.
MUM'S FURRY GLOVES

What a great idea, Gnasher!

TOWN HALL
UNUSUAL PET SHOW TODAY

Dennis's ten-legged dog is the winner!
Heh! Heh! Walter's red with rage, and his chameleon's green with envy!

# THE M-PLAN DIET

My Mum is always reading books on how to b thin, beautiful (Haw! Haw!) and healthy. All these books are soppy and full of pictures of people wearing daft leg-warmers, arm-warmers and bod warmers but no brain–warmers — which is what they need the most! Softies!

Here is a proper menacing diet book for menacing Mums. My Mum says it should carry a health warning, saying that it makes you look stup but what does she know?

If you want to be healthy you should eat lots of greens. I find the best way to do this is to use green food dye. That way you can have green steak, green custard and green chocolate.

Chewing your food properly is very important. If you want lessons on how to chew, my pet, Gnasher, will give you them for two bones per half hour. If you have a really big appetite my neighbour, Stanley Livingstone's crocodile, gives lessons in very advanced chewing. It is best if you go for a lesson when he is not hungry, though, because he has a very big mouth and bad eyesight.

My Mum says it is important to eat lots of fibre. I didn't know what this means but it doesn't mean man made fibre—even Rasher doesn't like the taste of nylon. Maybe the postman's trousers contain fibre though — Gnasher loves them.

Some people say that if you want to be brainy you should eat lots of fish. I don't think this can be true. Seals, for example, eat nothing but fish (they don't even have chips with it!) and they aren't too bright. I once tried to get one to do my homework and it only got two marks more than I usually get! Call that brainy?

# G PLAN DIET

THIS IS GNASHERS WAY OF KEEPING SLIM!

LIVE IN A KENNEL — IF YOU'RE TOO BIG YOU'RE FORCED TO SLIM

BURY YOUR FOOD — SO THAT IT'S SO MUCKY WHEN IT'S DUG UP IT'S INEDIBLE!

AND FINALLY — WEAR A MUZZLE — THIS NOT ONLY PREVENTS YOU EATING, IT STOPS YOU ASKING FOR THE MUZZLE TO BE REMOVED!

MUFFLED MUMBLING

# EXERCISES

PUSH-UPS

WE NEED A LADDER!

PUSH

STAR JUMPS

MUST SEE MY HERO, MR T.

CINEMA

"MR T"

JOGGING

I LOVE MESSING UP WALTER'S WORK.

JOG

YOGA

I DON'T KNOW WHICH BIT TO YELL AT!

# HEALTHY MEALS

ALPHABET SPAGHETTI — (RICH IN VITAMINS ABCDEFGHIJK, ETC, ETC.)

NAIL SOUP — (RICH IN IRON)

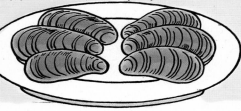

MUSSELS — (THESE MAKE YOU STRONG — AT LEAST IF YOU'RE AS BAD AT SPELLING AS I AM)

# The Key to Success

GOING FISHING, DENNIS?

YES!

FISHING IN THE HOUSE?

SNORE! SNORE!

ARE YOU AFTER DAD'S FALSE TEETH?

SNORE! GRUNT!

WHEE! GRUNT!

NOW FOR SOME FUN, OLD PAL!

GNASHER

LET'S HAVE A SUPER SCOFF!

LARDER

CLICK!

LATER—

OOPS! DAD'S FOUND OUT! LET'S HIDE!

ANGRY ROAR!

COAL CELLAR

BUT—

HEH-HEH! YOU CAN'T ESCAPE FROM CRAFTY OLD DAD!

HERE'S ONE KEY THAT YOU DIDN'T KNOW ABOUT! WILL YOU GO TO BED WITHOUT SUPPER, OR WILL YOU OPEN THE BOX?

ER— I'LL OPEN THE BOX!

TOUGH LUCK, DENNIS— YOU'VE WON THE BOOBY PRIZE! BEND OVER!

AGH!

OOYAH! YEEK! YAROOP!

DENNIS'S HOWLS SOUND A LITTLE OFF-**KEY!**

PLEASE, SIR, I'VE GOT MY OWN COLONY OF SILK WORMS!

HOW NICE!

YAH! YOU'RE THE SILKIEST WORM OF THE LOT, WALTER!

SILENCE, BOY! WE SHOULD ALL BE LIKE WALTER AND STUDY INSECTS.

I'M GOING TO WEAVE A SHAWL FOR MY MUMMY WITH THE SILK I GET FROM MY COLONY.

LATER, AT HOME—

I'VE CAUGHT ONE, GNASHER!

THUMP!

THUD!

SOON AFTER—

MUMMY WILL BE PLEASED WITH HER NICE SHAWL.

AHA!

WOULD YOU LIKE TO STUDY MY INSECTS?

WH- WHAT?

CHOMP!

CHEW!

GOBBLE!

MUNCH!

EEK! NASTY MOTHS!

ONE SECOND LATER—

SNIFFLE!

IT'S MORE LIKE A LACE CURTAIN THAN A SILK SHAWL!

LOOM

GNACKLE!

BACK HOME—

WALTER'S SURE TO TELL DAD, BUT DAD CAN'T SPANK ME WITH A CHEWED SLIPPER — EAT UP, MOTHS!

CRUNCH!

OOYAH! THIS SLIPPER'S TOO TOUGH TO CHEW!

SOON— ER— DAD, WHY DON'T YOU TAKE UP A NICE HOBBY LIKE ENTOMOLOGY?

NO, THANKS! I'M QUITE HAPPY WITH THE ONE I'VE GOT— SPANKINGOLOGY!

# GIVE A LITTLE "WHISTLE"

Pah! What a useless brute! Can't you teach him to do a useful job?

SNOOZSH!

DENNIS VISITS MR BLEAT, A WELL-KNOWN SHEPHERD —

I want to train Gnasher to be a sheepdog.

Right, lad. The orders are given by whistling.

Pay attention, Gnasher.

LATER, BACK HOME—

I'm training Gnasher to be a working dog, Dad!

Good! I'll put on the kettle for a cup of tea.

PHEEP!

Orders! I must round up the sheep!

PHEEP!

More orders! The sheep must be behind that hedge!

There they are! What do I do next?

PHEEP! PHEEP!

Aha! Order Number Three!

AT HOME—

I'd like to have this room carpeted from wall-to-wall with white woollen carpet.

Hmm! That would look nice, dear!

What's happening?

BAAA! BAAA! BAAA!

Gulp! It looks like Gnasher's bringing his work home!

Eek! Get them out!

BAA! MAA! BLEAT!

What are you bleating for, Mum? You've got what you wanted—a wall-to-wall woollen carpet!

# PISTOL PACKING MENACE

# PONY TALE

DENNIS IS WATCHING SHOW-JUMPING—

Harvey Broome is super!

Can I have a show-jumper, Dad?

Not likely! Show-jumpers cost hundreds of pounds! I couldn't afford to give you an old donkey!

LATER— Snigger! What do you think of my show-jumper, Dennis? We're off to the Gymkhana. I'm wearing my new, red hacking-jacket.

ENVIOUS

I'll see if I can borrow that pony Uncle Fred uses to pull the milk cart.

Erk! It's that menace who tried to make me into a bucking bronco when he was here on holiday! I'm off!

Bah! And he would have made a good show-jumper, too!

Come on, Ferdinand! You'll have to do!

AT THE GYMKHANA —

And in the lead at the moment is Walter on Twinkle-toes with a clear round in 55 seconds. And next to jump—Dennis the Menace on Ferdinand!

Gasp! Dennis the Menace and Ferdinand are eliminated!

Whoops! He's after Walter's red jacket!

BAH!  SMASH!  CRASH!

SNORT!

BACK HOME —

Mum's got a show-jumper for you to try out, Dennis.

Yahoo!

Do you like this new Fair Isle jumper? It's going on show at the Women's Guild knitting contest.

Gagh!

And now a lovely jumper modelled by a sweet little boy!

I'll never be able to look Harvey Broome in the eye again!

# KNIGHT-TIME STORY

*O*NCE upon a time in Ye Ancient town of Beanoium (now known as Beanotown), a youth by the name of Dennis the Knave was playing football outside a castle. Up on the castle wall he saw Ye Prince of Softies, a sickly youth by the name of Walter the Wet, plucking up the courage to look down. The Knave (which is what they called Menaces in those days) could not control himself. Before he knew what he was doing, he had kicked the ball at the Wet One. If he had known what he was doing, he'd have done exactly the same and might even have aimed his shot a bit better. As it was, he missed the ancient Softy and the ball carried on into the castle until the thud of ball on King was heard. As the King roared with anger The Knave marched into the castle.

"Pesky Prince! He must have moved — I never miss!" quoth Dennis. Soon the Knave came across the King who was angrily jumping up and down on his ball.

"Can I have my ball back?" ventured the Knave. The King was purple with rage — or possibly purple from jumping on the ball, it doesn't really matter — he was purple anyway.

"What?" howled the King, amazed at the Knave's cheek (or nose—that doesn't matter either). Then the King calmed down and smiled.

"Ah! You're 'Dennis the Knave' from 'Ye Beano'. I'm a great fan. I'll give you your ball back if you help me with a few things."

"OK. As long as it's not window cleaning," said the Knave. This puzzled the King, as windows had not been invented yet.

"No. It's not window cleaning. I want you to sort out that fight over there." He pointed to where a Knight and a dragon were chasing each other in circles. The King said angrily, "They've been at it for a month — the Queen can't get the washing hung out for all the smoke." Dennis whistled and in no time (well some time — but not much) a dog appeared.

SWISH!!

GNASH! GNASH!

JUMP

"See to it, good Gnasher." The dog growled at once. At the fearsome sound the dragon stopped in its tracks, screamed and then leapt into the arms of the Knight. He soon agreed to use only smokeless fuel once it had been invented.

The King took Dennis to the kitchens. "Look at all these pies, they're inedible — our cook is useless."

"No trouble — I'll just open the window," said Dennis going over to the shutter. "Oops! Forgot windows hadn't been invented yet." He opened the shutter, though, and a waft of pie scent issued fifth (a bit further than issuing forth). In even less time than it had taken Gnasher — which wasn't very long, you'll remember — Squire Pie-Face arrived.

"Verily I adore pies!'' he shouted and fell upon
the pies, (actually Dennis tripped him) eating
ravenously. In a trice (which is not a medieval
bicycle with no wheels) — the pies were gone and
all that was left was a sore stomach. ''Ye Groo!
Such a foul banquet!'' moaned Pie-Face, clutching
his tum.

''Don't worry I'll cure your stomach ache,'' spake
Dennis, who then asked to be brought the cook and
a suit of armour. When they arrived he told the
cook to get into the armour. Everyone looked
puzzled. Then Dennis told Gnasher to make a face.
At the sight of the terrifying countenance the
cook's knees began to knock wildly, making a
repeated loud clanging sound. Within minutes,
Pie-Face said he had such a bad headache that he
didn't notice his painful tum and left happily. The
King cried ''Stop that racket!''

CLANG! CLANG!

THROB  THROB

FIERY

BLAST

SIZZLE!

Dennis smiled, ''No problem — I'll even kill two
birds with one stone.'' He picked up a vat of
custard. ''This stuff looks horrible — you'll want rid
of it.'' The King agreed. Dennis then poured the
custard into the cook's armour. As it filled up it
muffled the knocking. The King was still worried
though.

''What will I do about cooking now?'' Dennis
looked outside and saw the Knight and the dragon
shaking hands. This gave the Knave an idea. Soon
the Knight and his new friend were in the kitchens.
The Knight wore a chef's hat and toasted bread by
the dragon's breath.

''Since we've given up fighting this'll be an ideal
job for us.'' The dragon nodded in agreement and
singed the Knight from head to toe.

**BURST**

"Thanks for all you've done — I'm going to solve my final problem and make you my new wizard. The last one turned the Queen into a frog. She looks better, but the croaking keeps me awake at night." The old wizard was angry — yea, exceedingly angry. He didn't want to lose his job because he loved wearing stupid hats and daft cloaks. Unhappily Berlin (he was a distant German cousin of Merlin) handed over his garments. After putting them on, Dennis took his ball from the King and resumed his game of football. He soon found out the reason why no famous footballers wear wizards' hats. After going up to head the sphere, he came down with the ball punctured and stuck on the end of his hat. Berlin rolled about laughing as Dennis fumed. But before long Berlin had stopped laughing because Dennis reached for his magic wand.

PING!
PING!

**BLAST**

"Wah! He's going to turn me into something nasty!" wailed Berlin as he ran away. Dennis didn't though. His wand was a hollow one and it made an excellent peashooter, so he peppered Berlin with peas as he chased him. (Peppered peas were a great delicacy in olden days). "Pesky hat — ruined my game!" moaned Dennis. The King was perplexed.

"Hmm! Can't have the Knave running about with that peashooter every time he bursts a ball." So the King called the royal hatter — "Make me a wizard's hat that won't puncture a football!"

Soon the hatter produced his creation. Instead of one big cone it had lots of small rubber ones.

"What a wondrous creation!" enthused Dennis the Knave.

And that is why, to this day, the ancestors of Dennis the Knave comb their hair into the style of the ancient wizard's hat.

# "MONKEY" BUSINESS

PICADILLY'S CIRCUS CHIMPANZEE MISSING— £5 REWARD FOR ITS RETURN.

Let's catch the chimp and get that reward, Gnasher!

SO—

This should trap the hairy rascal!

MONKEY NUTS

BUT—

Grr! Get lost, squirrel— you're not a chimp!

BACK HOME—

Bah! That pesky squirrel ate all our chimp-bait! Oho! . . .

AND—

Heh! Heh! With that "bald-wig" we used last week, you look just like a monkey, Gnasher!

Gnunk! Gnunk!

SO—

A BIT SHORT-SIGHTED

Here's your chimp, Mr Picadilly!

Great work, lad! Here's your reward.

BUT—

Gasp! Where did that dog come from? And where's my chimp?

TOSS

Come on, Gnasher—I'll buy you a pile of bones, and—Hey!

SNATCH

Grr! Come back with our reward, you little monkey!

Unk! Unk!

PICADILLY'S CIRCUS

I'll be safe in my nice cosy cage!

£5

Give us the reward, Mr Picadilly— we made the chimp come back!

I'm keeping the money— that'll teach you not to make a monkey out of me!

PICADILLY'S CIRCUS

Gnash-Gnunk!

Gnook-Growl!

HOW DID THESE MONKEYS GET ON THIS PAGE? OH, IT'S ONLY DENNIS AND GNASHER IN A BAD MOOD!

# LAUGHTER LINES

IN ENGLISH CLASS—

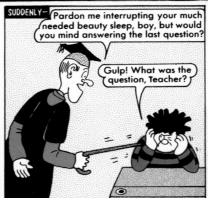

SUDDENLY—

Pardon me interrupting your much needed beauty sleep, boy, but would you mind answering the last question?

Gulp! What was the question, Teacher?

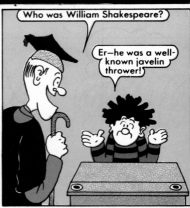

Who was William Shakespeare?

Er—he was a well-known javelin thrower!

Impudent imbecile! You will do one hundred "lines"!

AT FOUR O' CLOCK—

Don't forget to have those hundred "lines" here for me to see tomorrow, Dennis!

H'm!

PRESENTLY—

Aha! I've got an idea, Gnasher!

SO—

Come back with my sandwiches!

THEN—

Tally-ho!

DENNIS'S SCHOOL

NEXT MORNING—

I hope you've done these lines, Dennis.

Yes, teacher.

DENNIS'S SCHOOL

Do you want to count them?

Gasp!

NOW DENNIS AND GNASHER ARE MAKING BEE-LINES FOR THE HORIZON—

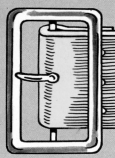

# KEEPING
## —GNASHER'S GUIDE

Dogs should always be well fed.

They should get plent[y]

Give your dog a roomy kennel —
even if you have to do without.

Don't let your dog get bored.

Make sure his collar fits.

All dogs should

of exercise.

Always give them a bedtime story.

Don't let your pup strain himself.

Make sure your dog's hair is tidy
— when it's on the floor.

ave name tags.

And — most important — give him his own "Beano".

# SLIDE SHOW

GNASHER AND I HAVE SET UP A NEW WORLD RECORD FOR SLIDING DOWN THE BANISTERS, READERS!

STOP WATCH

HERE WE GO!

TICK! TICK!

I'M LOOKING FORWARD TO THESE SAUSAGES. I EVEN MANAGED TO KEEP THEM AWAY FROM THAT DREADFUL DOG!

BUT—

OOOOOH!

GANGWAY, DAD!

CHOMPSH! CHOMPSH!

# DRIVEN UP THE POLE

Coo! This is super! All about polar-bear hunting!

I'm going to be an eskimo and hunt polar-bears!

AT THE ZOO —
ZOO
OPEN DAILY — DAWN TILL DUSK
Psst!

No—I certainly won't swop a polar-bear for a white mouse! Go away!

Where can I get a polar-bear?

BACK HOME—
Now pretend to be a polar-bear, Gnasher!
FLOUR

Aha! I've got you cornered on that big iceberg!

Shriek! What's been going on?
Glurk! It's Mum!

Gnush, masher! I mean, mush, Gnasher!

MUSEUM
Let's hide in here!

SUSPICIOUS GLARE
ESKIMOS HUNTING POLAR-BEAR
LOOKS LIKE OUR ESKIMO PALS ARE GOING TO GET A FROSTY RECEPTION!

# IT'S A SMALL WORLD

I'm putting Foo-foo in for a dog-show! He's sure to win!

Not at all! Gnasher will win!

HANDSOME

Snigger! Gnasher can't enter for that—but Foo-foo's a miniature poodle!

MINI-DOG SHOW MINIATURE DOGS ONLY

If I give Gnasher a good wash, maybe he'd shrink!

SO—

SPLASH!
WOW!
GNASH!
GURGLE!

WHOOSH!

LATER—

Bah! Gnasher hasn't shrunk but my clothes have!

Try some of Mum's reducing biscuits, Gnasher, and see if they reduce you!

BUT THE ONLY THING THAT'S REDUCED IS MUM—SHE'S REDUCED TO A FIT OF RAGE—

Put my biscuits back at once!

LATER, IN DENNIS'S SHED —

I've just had a great idea!

Repeat after me, "Bow—wow!"

AT THE MINI-DOG SHOW —

Amazing! Dennis,s dog is the winner!

Bow wow!

Pst! Don't tell anybody, it's just my highly-trained hairy-caterpillar, Harold!

# CHARMED I'M SURE!

GEOGRAPHY LESSON —

YES, SNAKE-CHARMERS CAN BE SEEN IN THE BAZAARS OF INDIA.

I'D LIKE TO TRY THAT.

MEANWHILE, WALTER IS NOT SO KEEN —

OOER! I'M SSSCARED OF SSSNAKES!

HISSS!

YEEK! THERE'S A SNAKE BEHIND ME!

IT WAS JUST ME, WALTER! I THOUGHT YOU'D BE PALS WITH SNAKES BEING A LITTLE REPTILE YOURSELF! YAH! HISSSS!

OOO! HOW NASTY YOU ARE, DENNIS!

BACK HOME—

AH! MY TRUSTY TIN WHISTLE!

ALL I NEED NOW IS A SNAKE AND I'M IN BUSINESS!

TOWEL

PET SHOP

AH, COME TO MY ARMS, MY BEAUTY!

DENNIS, UNTIE THAT PYTHON AND PUT IT BACK!

AW, I JUST WANTED IT FOR A WEEK'S FREE TRIAL!

SO—

I'LL PRACTISE MY PLAYING.

BUT—

GET OUT OF IT! THIS IS MY FAVOURITE PLAYING SPOT!

HUH! I'M NOT GETTING ON FAR WITH MY NEW CAREER, BUT, IF I CAN'T GET A SNAKE, WHAT CAN I USE? AH! I'VE GOT AN IDEA!

SOON—

SSSS!

A FOO-FOO WALTER'S CURIOUS POODLE

LOOK AT HIM DANCE!

NOOGH!

SPLASH!

LATER—

WHAT'S ALL THIS MISCHIEF I HEAR YOU'VE BEEN UP TO, BOY?

I HAVEN'T BEEN UP TO MISCHIEF, DAD! IN FACT I'VE BEEN CHARMING ALL DAY!

THAT'S NOT QUITE THE WORD I'D USE TO DESCRIBE YOUR BEHAVIOUR.

# EASY AS PIE

RECIPE TIME WITH DENNIS'S PAL PIE-FACE

I WILL NOW SHOW YOU HOW EASY IT IS TO GET A DELICIOUS PIE!

PUT — AHEM! — YOUR PASTRY IN A CIRCULAR DISH!

THROW

FLOP!

THEN TRIM YOUR PASTRY—

CEMENT POWDER

GNASH! GNASH!

—UNTIL IT'S SET HARD!

SHAKE

CLUNK!

NOW FIX YOUR PIE TO YOUR CARTIE—

# SWELL STORY

GRANNY'S LOOKING GRIMMER THAN USUAL. WHAT'S THE TROUBLE?

Ooyah! I've got a swollen bunion. I can't get my shoe on!

The only thing I can wear is the Demon Whacker.

That's the Whacker out of action—now for some fun!

WHACKER'S BOX

GRANNY'S PRIZE ORNAMENT

You young whelp! If only I could chase you!

IN THE BUTCHER'S SHOP—

A pound of tripe, please. It's an old wives' tale that tripe and onions are good for bunions.

Slurp! My bunions feel better already!

I'll just leave it to cool for a minute!

Slurpsh! Tripe and onions!

Agh! That boy has let his hound out of control! I've warned him before!

You'll pay for this, laddie!

Eh?

HOBBLE

THE CHASE GOES DOWN TO THE SEA-SHORE—

HOBBLE

SPLOSH!

Yahoo! I'm cured! Now I can catch Dennis!

Yes, salt water's very good for curing aches and pains!

DOCTOR PROCTOR, OUT FOR A STROLL

PAINLESS

LATER—

Yes, readers, you guessed it.— Granny managed to catch me!

ACHE!

# DENTURE VENTURE

A NEW BULL-DOG HAS ARRIVED NEXT DOOR—

There's going to be a big fight! Better get Gnasher into strict training!

GURR! GNASH!

SO, GNASHER STARTS TRAINING—

Hup! Hup! Hup!

AT MEALTIME— One slimming dog biscuit— and no bones about it till the fight's over!

Groansh!

IN THE PARK—

TRIGGER    FAMOUS GUN DOG

A bone!

SLURPSH!

GNASH!    SOLID MARBLE

LEAP    TRIGGER

THEN—

Har! My enemy— and unarmed, too!

GUMMY

BITE    SNAP!    MUNCH!

SLURP! SLURP! SUCK!

ONE DEFEAT LATER—

I must get new fangs!

AT GRANNY'S HOUSE—

HOME SWEET HOME

I'll borrow Granny's fangs!

BACK INTO BATTLE—

Give him the old one-two, Gnasher!

THEN—

Well done, champ! But you've lost a few teeth in the battle!

SCREECH!

LOOKS LIKE GNASHER'S GOT ANOTHER FIGHT ON HIS HANDS!

TOP DOG

EIGHT O'CLOCK— ...YES, IT'S BREAKFAST IN BED TODAY.

HOW KIND—I'D BETTER GET BACK TO BED.

MUCH LATER— HMPH! WHERE'S MY BREAKFAST IN BED GOT TO?

Home Sweet Home

MEANWHILE— EAT UP, OLD FRIEND! THIS IS THE BIG DAY~ THE DAY OF THE WORLD BONE-GNASHING CHAMPIONSHIP!

OFF YOU GO FOR A GENTLE TROT ROUND THE HOUSE TO KEEP YOUR APPETITE UP~ BUT DON'T TIRE YOURSELF OUT!

EH?

GNASH!

HEY! GET YOUR LEG OUT OF MY GNASHER'S PRECIOUS MOUTH, POSTMAN!

GURR!

GURR!

WHO'LL BE FIRST TO THE FEED?

START

1

2

3

4

5

6

ZOOM!

4. THE MENACES STOPPED BY SCENTED FLOWER-BED. THROW AN EVEN NUMBER TO ESCAPE THE SMELL, THEN TAKE YOUR TURN.

28

27

29. THE MENACES GET A LIFT ON LORRY — FORWARD 3.

29

30

31

32

PONG

HORRIBLE NIFF

26. BILLY WHIZZ'S SLIPSTREAM BLASTS SOFTIES FORWARD 4.

26

25

24. THE MENACES PAUSE FOR CATAPULT PRACTICE — MISS A TURN.

33. THE MENACES' DADS WAITING — THEY DASH BACK 2.

33

34

35. THE SOFTIES TAKE THEIR AFTERNOON NAP — THEY SLEEP THROUGH THEIR TURN.

35

36

37

37. SOFTIES JOIN GIRLS FOR SKIPPING GAME — MISS A TURN.

# GET YOUR "SKATES" ON

# NOT YETI!

MEANWHILE, WALTER IS ALL ATREMBLE —

OH! I CAN'T BEAR TO WATCH!

AFTER THE FILM —

BEST LAUGH I'VE HAD FOR AGES!

OOER! MUMSY, THAT WAS RATHER FRIGHTENING!

SHAKE

THEN —

SHRIEK! IT'S A YETI!

THERE, THERE, DIDDUMS! IT'S ONLY A SWEET LITTLE DOGGUMS!

BACK HOME —

I'LL PLAY A PRANK ON WALTER!

GNESH!

I'LL BORROW MUM'S FUR COAT!

AT WALTER'S —

WHIMPER! I'M SCARED OF THE DARK, MUMMY!

DON'T WORRY, WATTIE—I'LL LEAVE A NIGHT-LIGHT.

SUDDENLY —

EEK! IT'S GONE ALL DARK!

SPURT!

ROAR!

SCREECH! IT'S A YETI! SAVE ME, MUMMY!

OUTSIDE WALTER'S HOUSE —

GNESH!

HO-HO! DID YOU SEE THE LOOK ON WALTER'S FACE, GNASHER?

SUDDENLY—

WHAT ARE YOU UP TO, BOY?

ERKSH!

YEEK!

DENNIS'S DAD

I'M NOT FRIGHTENED OF THE HORRIBLE SIGHT OUT THERE! IN FACT, I'M QUITE ENJOYING IT!

WHAP!

YEOWL!

ARGAAAH!

WHOP!

# LOLLY FOLLY

# COAT OF MANY COLOURS

# "REED" THIS!

Basketwork today, class.

Groan!

Place the canes in buckets of water to soften them.

Don't put Walter in the bucket, Dennis!

Squeek!

I forgot— He's soft enough already!

Gurr!

LATER— Hmm! We've run out of canes. We'll go to the reed beds and gather some more.

Very good, Gnasher!

AT THE RIVER—

Go and pull some reeds and weave baskets from them.

What's this then?

Oh, how clever, Dennis! You've made that lovely basket already!

Gulp! It's even got fish in it! How do you explain that?

Who pinched my basket?

Gulp! It's Dad!

I haven't got my slipper— but never mind!

Look—a cane-slipper— twice as stingy!

Groan!

# Tinker? Tailor? Soldier? Sailor

## WHAT WILL DENNIS BE WHEN HE GROWS UP?

**AN ARCHITECT?**

ER — NOT QUITE WHAT I HAD IN MIND!

**A SIGN PAINTER?**

I HATE SOFTIES

B-BUT I ONLY WANTED YOU TO WRITE "BUTCHER"!

**A LAWYER?**

MY CLIENT PLEADS NOT GUILTY TO EXCESSIVE PIE-SCOFFING!

SNORE!

WITNESS BOX

**A TEACHER?**

WELL DONE, TEACHER'S PET!

PAT PAT

# GETTING THE WIND UP

"It's right what they say, "The March winds doth blow"!"

This is great kite-flying weather, Gnasher—we'll enter for that!

GRAND CHILDRENS' KITE CONTEST — TODAY — SPECIAL PRIZE FOR THE HIGHEST FLYER!

THUMP!

What's that noise, Gnasher?

Huh—that noise must have been the wind dropping!

CALM AND SERENE

Bah! This is no use!

THEN— You point this out the window, Gnasher.

BLOW

SUCK — BLOW

Whoopee! This is great!

Eeek! Get outside, you pesky pup!

Bah! Mum's switched it off!

We'll go and see Uncle Fred who works at the aerodrome.

AT THE AERODROME—

WHOOSH!

WIND TUNNEL

OUTLET PIPE

Yippee! I've got permission to fly my kite beside the wind tunnel!

UP IN SKYBLOB, THE SPACE-CRAFT—

Corks! Look at that! Report back to base!

THIS SIDE UP

SKYBLOB

BACK ON EARTH—

And there wasn't even any wind! How did you do it, Dennis?

Sheer skill, lads— what else?

DAILY BLARE

LOCAL MENACE BREAKS WORLD KITE FLYING ALTITUDE RECORD BY 250,000,000 FEET

# GRAND 'BAND'

Now to spend a tranquil hour listening to Beethoven.

SUDDENLY—
SCREECH! CLATTER! RAT-TAT! CRASH!
What's that?

CLASH! BUZZ! RAT-TAT!

What's the meaning of this racket?
We've always wanted to play in a band!

I know the band-master—I'll see if I can get you lot into the band.
THINKS: At least they'll be out of my hair!
Thanks, Dad!

AT BAND PRACTICE—
Ok, Dennis, you can have a trombone—Walter, you can play the big drum, and Curly, you can play the oompah.

ATER—
Ah! Back to Beethoven.
GENTLE TRILLING

SUDDENLY—
PAA-RAA!
THUMP!

Sorry, Dad! I must practise. We're in the big parade on Saturday.
Good lad, Dennis! To think a son of mine is appearing in a big parade!

SO—
I'm off to the parade. I'm meeting Curly and Walter behind the bandstand at two.
We'll be there to see the parade, and we're bringing all our friends.

Heh-heh! I'm the fastest bandsman in the west!

BUT—
CRUMP!
BASH!
CLANG!
PAN WITH HIS PIPES    PAN WITH HIS PIPES

AND WHEN THE PARADE PASSES—
OOMPAH!
SHAME
RATTLE
CLASH
BUZZZ

# DIVE, DIVE, DIVE!

I'M GOING TO TEACH YOU TO DIVE PROPERLY.

TO THE BATHS →

DENNIS IS SUPPOSED TO BE BANNED— BUT I'LL LET HIM IN AS HE'S ACCOMPANIED BY A RESPONSIBLE ADULT. THAT PERISHING PUP STAYS OUT!

← POOL

SAUNA →

SOON—

YAHOO!

GERONIMO!

PYON-N-N-G!

BLOOMPH!

EXCUSE ME DROPPING IN LIKE THIS, WALTER!

BLAD-DOOMPH!

WALTER

# COME TO SUNNY

PUBLISHED BY THE BEANOTOWN TOURIST OFFICE

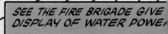

# BEANOTOWN

SEE BEANOTOWN MUSEUM...

...OR VISIT DAD'S MUSEUM.

I CONFISCATED THIS WHEN DENNIS WAS TWO!

AMMO

AMMO

FLOUR BOMB

INK PELLETS

EN WATCH THE MENACES PROPERLY.

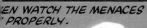

PPLE

FAKE BUILDING

SWOOSH!

VISIT AN ARCHEOLOGICAL SITE...

BEGUN 1949

...OR SEE THE SPEEDED UP VERSION.

WHERE'S MY BONE?

SEE THE ART GALLERY...

ZZZ

SNORE

YAWN!

...OR LOOK AT OTHER PICTURES.

THIS IS WHAT HE LOOKED LIKE, OFFICER.

HERE'S THE CULPRIT'S PHOTOGRAPH.

# WIZARD BLIZZARD

GOSH! MUM MUST HAVE MADE A SNOWMAN THAT LOOKS LIKE DAD!

GRR!

SHAKE

GULP! IT **IS** DAD!

POOR DAD! HE FORGOT ABOUT THE ICE! HE CERTAINLY "SLIPPED UP" THERE! HEE-HEE!

LATER—

THERE HE IS! WE'VE SOME OLD SCORES TO SETTLE WITH YOU FROM LAST YEAR, MENACE!

QUICK, GNASHER—ROLL OVER!

LOOK OUT! HE'S HOLDING A GIANT SNOWBALL!

HELP! RUN FOR IT!

TEE-HEE! THAT SCARED THEM!

THEN—

WHY DON'T YOU MAKE A PROPER SLIDE LIKE THIS, WALTER?

OH, NO, I COULDN'T— THEY ARE AGAINST PARK REGULATIONS!

SLIDE

HERE I COME! WHEE!

KEEP POLISHING, GNASHER!

HELP! I'M SLIPPING!

OOF!

GULP! IT'S DAD! THAT'S DONE IT!

GNASHULP!

LOOK AT SOPPY DENNIS BUILDING A SNOW-CHAIR! SNIGGER! TITTER!

AH! THAT'S MUCH COOLER!

TEE-HEE! NOW I SEE WHY HE WANTED A SNOW-CHAIR!

# TRANCE — NO CHANCE!

Ok, Dad, we're ready to go to the concert.

No dogs allowed!

Aw, Dad!

I think I'll wear my duffel coat— It's a bit chilly.

Hurry up!

AT THE CONCERT—

You can take your coat off, Dennis.

No thanks, Dad. I'm quite comfortable.

Whisper :— Enjoying the show, Gnasher?

Gnash!

A HYPNOTIST DOES HIS ACT—

You will obey my every word!

HYPNOTISED

There's an idea for keeping Dennis in order!

LATER—

Here you are, sir. "Hypnotism for Beginners".

I don't like the look of this!

I'll fool Dad! First, I need an old ping-pong ball!

CHOP

LATER—

You are in my power! You will obey my every word! You will do your homework!

I will obey, Master!

UP IN DENNIS'S BEDROOM—

Never mind the homework! Let's get on with studying "The Beano"!

LATER —

Your son has failed to do his homework again!

What? He can't have!

I don't know why, but I never seem to see eye-to-eye with Dennis!

Snigger! Little does he know!

# WHAT A MOUTHFUL

DENNIS IS BORED AND RESTLESS—

ZONK!

Let's go and watch Mum in the kitchen.

I'm entertaining the Ladies' Circle to-night. I'll make the cake now and the sandwiches later so they'll be fresh.

Can we taste the cake-mix, Mum?

Paws off, you two!

SLOOP!

Out you go!

KLICK

LATER—

You've been a naughty boy, Dennis! Off you go to bed with no supper! I want you out of the way before the ladies arrive.

Aw, Mum! Just one sandwich and I promise to be a good boy for ever and ever!

Very well—but just one.

SO—

Now to make one sandwich.

Now that's what I call a sandwich!

CHOMP!

GNASH!

Eek! There's nothing left for the ladies! Dad—fetch your slipper!

NO IT'S NOT ANOTHER SUPER-SANDWICH. IT'S A PILE OF CUSHIONS WITH DENNIS SITTING ON TOP!